The seven Indian Chakras through the vision of Kabbalah

MEDITATION SERIES

INTRODUCTION

There is a belief in mystical Judaism that the Indian Vedas were descended from the children of Abraham with the slave Quetura who is one of his women after Sara's death. The children that Abraham had with this woman emigrated to India and gave rise to the religion of the Vedas carrying books of magic by Abraham, powerful books that gave rise to deep mystical knowledge within Indian culture.

There are many connections pointing to this, including the name of Brahma, the oldest and most powerful God in India who has a resemblance to the name Abraham, and Abraham. The goddess Sarasvati, wife of Brahma also has the same name as Sarah, wife of Abraham. She gave birth to Sara Kali who is the main goddess of the Roma people who emigrated from India hundreds of years ago.

This connection between Indians and Israelis is revealed in more depth in the connection between the Indian religion and the kabbalah. Kabbalah, a mystical knowledge of Judaism, has meditation techniques and believes in the plurality of inhabited worlds like in India.

At the time of Abraham, there were many forms of magic inherited from ancient peoples and Abraham had access to these formulas, to these mystical books of magic and passed this knowledge on to the slave's children who emigrated to India, because he feared that they were idolatry and therefore they passed on to Isaac and Ishmael.

This work addresses the important link that exists between the Indian Chakras and the Sephira of Sephiroth showing a common bond between Indian religion and Hebrew Kabbalah.

Just as Chakras are an important knowledge within the Indian religion, Sephiroth is the essence of Kabbalah, the most mystical and deepest part of Judaism.

Chakras are vortexes of energy that connect our physical body with the soul and influence the physical, as they are on important organs of the human body radiating energy that spreads through the body and defines our life, our daily lives.

It is the energy of the Chakras that radiated activates the organs and glands of the body mainly through the Coronal Chakra that pours its energy over the top of the head, over the pineal gland and the pituitary system, limbic system and the cerebral cortex.

At the top of the head this energy emanates from our divine self and through the aforementioned brain organs they control the whole body, both our gland system and the energy that flows throughout the nervous system.

It is this energy that is worked on in acupuncture, an invisible energy that Western science does not yet understand. Until recently this alternative science of acupuncture was pursued, blocked, but now this holistic knowledge is beginning to be released to the western world.

It is through the chakras that the exchange of energy occurs in which our spiritual body controls the soul and from the soul this control reaches the physical.

CHAPTER I

MEET THE 7 INDIAN CHAKRAS

First we will get to know them according to Indian culture and then understand the connection of the cabal with these Chakras according to the Sephiroth science of Jewish mysticism.

It is important to know that there is no Indian, Jewish or Arabic knowledge, everything is part of the universal knowledge that is compartmentalized within each culture, within each religion and that in fact is unique knowledge as Jung studied.

Jung discovered that the culture of various peoples is part of a universal knowledge that was formed with our daily experience and our contact with the supernatural world, but this knowledge is complemented despite presenting different views.

1) Crown Chakra;

At the top of the head, connected to the pineal gland. He is the main Chakra, because it is the crown, the head, receives everything that comes from the divine and decodes it, passing it to the other Chakras.

2) Frontal chakra.

On the forehead, it is connected to the third eye. He sees everything, for he unites the pineal with the pituitary and the hypothalamus forming the golden triangle of power, the postulant's spiritual vision.

3) Larynx chakra.

Located in the larynx it is linked to speech, the magic of speech, to the divine verb. It is activated when we do meditation using the Mantra and then this Chakra radiates the focus of meditation throughout the body.

4) Heart chakra.

As you are saying, it is the heart chakra linked to feeling and love. Within Kabbalah it is one of the main ones, as it determines our choices.

5) Solar plexus chakra.

This Chakra is very important for exchanging energy between worlds and dimensions.

6) Sacral chakra.

Linked to sexual energies, without it man cannot act in the world generating his offspring and leaving offspring, that's why this Chakra is very important, without him the human race would not even exist.

7) Base chakra.

Located at the base of the column is where the earth's energies, telluric and has connection with our past lives, our lower astral connected to worlds, dimensions and time.

Whoever manages to develop this Chakra receives super powers. Only observing that we enumerate the Chakras from top to bottom, from the head to the base of the column, but in Kabbalah we will invert becoming the first Chakra at the base of the column and the last at the head. This is common in esotericism, the inversion of the order of the Chakras.

CHAPTER II

THE CHAKRA BASE, ROOT OR MULADHARA

This Chakra is at the base of the spine and connects with the energy that comes from the earth. It is linked to the Kundalini energy, which in Western mysticism is the telluric energy that comes from the earth and is stored by the organism in this Chakra.

This Chakra was used by Ha Satan in Eden to tempt Eve and for him Satan climbed up the column and managed to install himself on the human backbone controlling humanity, all of humanity had this control and remains under control. Only Yeshua overcame the serpent in death so he was crucified, for the cross symbolizes victory over death, victory over the serpent.

The cross also symbolizes the 4 states of magic, terrestrial, aerial, water and fire magic and the death of the Messiah on the cross gave rise to the 4 gospels overcoming the 4 worlds of magic.

This happened even before the Adamic race, because we know that the Adamic race was the fifth race, since the beginning, since the first Ha Satan race controls man entering this Chakra. However Yeshua came to overcome the serpent, for it is written that one will be born who will step on the serpent's head. This one is Yeshua; he also acts in this Chakra through the tribe of Judah and Archangel Mikael and prevents the serpent from controlling the human species.

It is through this root Chakra that the confrontation between light and chaos begins and in this place is installed the energy vortex of Mikael for the fight against chaos.

In Sephiroth this Chakra is represented by Yesod, the foundation, since the root Chakra is the foundation of the human micro cosmos. Yesod is the new Sephira, as he understands that in Sephiroth the vortexes of energy start from the bottom up. The tenth Sephira is Malkuth represented by the feet; the new Sephira is the foundation, Yesod, also the root Chakra and the main point of Yeshua's action as a transforming element of the human species blocking the serpent's strength.

These are the main Chakras, but in this work we have to approach other Chakras to close with the Sephiroth, because as we have already mentioned there are hundreds of Chakras or points of energy.

sexta-feira, 10 de agosto de 2012

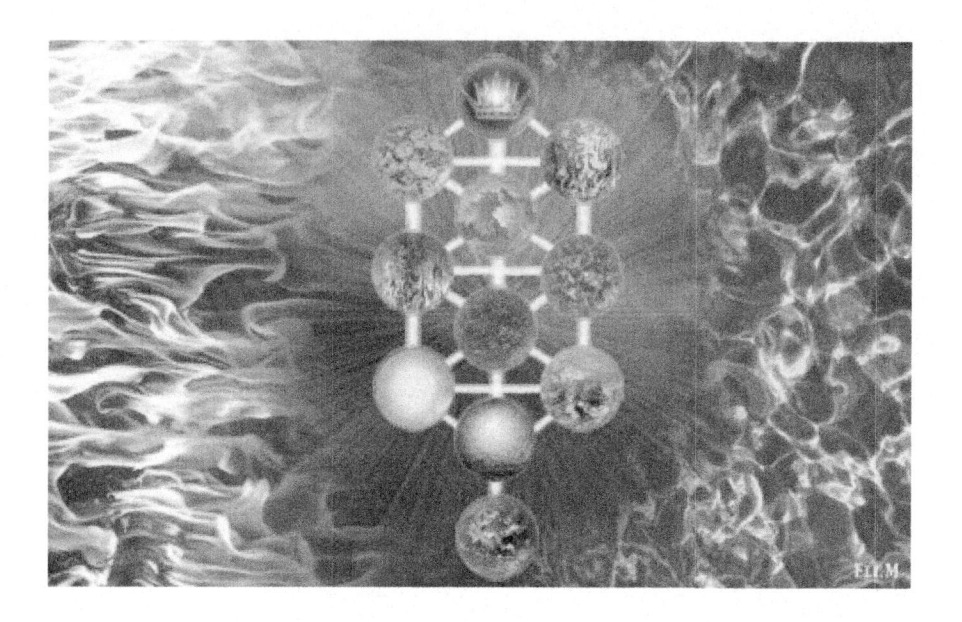

       Many sincere Kabbalists call Sephira Yesod the formation of the firmament because it is in it that the Creative Light gains this static form called the astral-physical plane; it is also in it that the Light is most veiled as possible, hidden from the view of those who have not awakened in themselves the spiritual nature ("the eyes of seeing").

But this is a reality of Sefirah before the angelic and human fall. Especially before the human fall, Sefirah Yesod was the greatest densification of the Light that we could find in the universe. But with the advent of the human fall, Yesod ceased to be the greatest dense manifestation of the Light, leaving this mission of densification to Sefirah Malkuth. This in turn is Sefirah Da'at - Spiritual Knowledge - which with the fall was forced to leave its place of origin in man and also in the universe - microcosms and macrocosms "The Lord God, therefore, threw him out of the garden from Eden, to plow the land from which he was taken." (Genesis 3: 23). This is confirmed in the Holy Scriptures: "And to Adam he said, Because you have listened to the voice of your wife, and have eaten of the tree of which I commanded you, saying, You shall not eat of it, cursed is the land because of you; in pain you shall eat of it all the days of your life (Gen 3:17)

With the fall Yesod assumed the role of entrance and exit door to the Garden of Eden, it is through Yesod that we enter the inner world of the heart - the spiritual center - through it we enter and leave our inner environment, the temple of the Spirit. Yesod is the door through which God has access to our heart and we have access to the Heart of God. The holy scriptures tell us: "And when he threw away the man, he put cherubs in the east of the garden of Eden, and a fiery sword that walked around, to guard the way of the tree of life. (Gen 3:24). These cherubs they are charged with blinding humanity so that they do not see or hear what is evident in the whole cosmos: The Real Truth.

Only with spiritual awakening can we enter by Yesod, only with the development of our spiritual senses do we gain access and by entering we will be in a new world where intense work on ourselves will begin, which is the replacement of our ephemeral will by the Will of the Father.

As it is also written: "And because the door is narrow, and the path that leads to life is narrow, and there are few who can find it." (Matthew 7: 14) and "Strive to enter through the narrow door; for I tell you that many will seek to enter, and will not be able to." (Luke 13:24) Yesod is the narrow door, the Sefirah that gives access to the inner world of spiritual symbolisms and it is only when we are becoming familiar with these symbols that spiritual maturity happens. In the densest planes, the Christic Spiritual Light takes on more and more veiling forms of His true essence, reaching the point of manifesting itself only under rustic symbols and here comes the importance of understanding the spiritual symbols to guide the Christian Way.

Performing Yesod, that is, understanding the spiritual symbolisms, the call to the high, the help of the

Transcendental Life - the sacrifice of Christ the cross - the Kabbalist enters the spiritual age of his soul, ceasing to live only for the personal and transitory rudiments for live the eternal values of the spirit.

http://misteriocristalino.blogspot.com/2012/08/sephira-yesod-porta-de-entrada-e-saida.html

As I mentioned this S ephira is where the initial fall occurred and with that Yeshua had to install his base in this region to contain the power of the Dragon.

Satan's power started there and then built another base in the human heart at Sephira Daath where he began to dispute with the Creator, alongside the Sephira of the heart, the control of man's senses, blowing in his mind the temptation and revolt against the Creator .

It all started at Sephira Root, then the human drama of the original fall began both in the Adamic race and before it.

In Indian science this Sephira is represented by a cross, as it symbolizes the cross of Yeshua where he blocked the serpent's power over the human mind.

Just as Moses lifted up the serpent in the desert, the son of man was lifted up on the cross to overcome the power of the serpent.

The bronze serpent symbolizes this telluric energy, the control over the human soul from Sephira Yesod and the Root Chakra, but the Messiah paid the price by blocking the force of Ha Satan and purifying the human soul, both the soul and the body, because the Chakras make the connection between the soul and the body and with that the bronze serpent that Moshe raised in the universe and that symbolized the energy of the angels to control the serpent was replaced by the energy of Yeshua the Messiah.

He replaced the bronze serpent by stepping on the serpent's head and when the Ram won the serpent the whole earth was amazed.

The ram symbolizes Yeshua, but Lucifer also pretends to be a ram to deceive the human race and tries to take Yeshua's place by creating Mitra and the worship of Sunday as sacred, so Christianity says that Sunday is sacred.

This power to twist the truth and try to imitate the true eternal lamb has led humanity to the edge of the abyss, but a spiritual revolt will happen to once again block the strength of the serpent that insists on controlling humanity.

CHAPTER III

THE SPLENIC CHAKRA

The second Chakra is the Splenic Chakra located near the spleen. It is a dangerous Chakra because it is connected to the abyss, the second dimension and that is why Indian Yogis avoid developing this Chakra because of the dangerous energies involved in it. This Chakra is called the Solar Plexus Chakra and I inverted it because the second Chakra should be the umbilical, but I invested, because this Chakra is connected to the second dimension, to the abyss.

At Sephiroth this Chakra is represented by Sephira Hod. This Sephira is passive, feminine, it means glory and splendor and it is the Sephira linked to the astral body. In the astral body there are many desires and feelings linked to the limbic system of the brain and for this reason it is a complicated Chakra.

There are several levels of the astral body, that is, several astral bodies and in this Sephira there are several astral bodies trying to come into evidence in the human body.

In the spleen chakra is where Yeshua received the spear hole and blood and water flowed when it was punctured at this location. This spear hole is connected to the Church, the salvation of the Gentiles, because Adam also had a hole in the side and from a rib extracted from him Eve was created, in the same way when Yeshua was pierced in the side by the spear appeared to the church.

That is why Hod symbolizes the woman, the feminine, the passive who is silent, but is able to act through this silence and achieve great achievements.

Behold, your people among you are like women; the doors of your land will be completely open to your enemies; fire will consume your bolts.

Draw water for the siege, strengthen your strongholds; it enters the mud, and steps on the clay, takes the form for the bricks.

The fire there will consume you, the sword will exterminate you; it will consume you, like the locust. Multiply like the locust, multiply like the locusts.

You have multiplied your merchants more than the stars in the sky; the locust will spread and fly.

Your princes are like locusts, and your captains are like large locusts, who camp in the hedges on cold days; when the sun rises, they fly, so that the place where they are is no longer known.

Your shepherds will sleep, O king of Assyria, your illustrious ones will rest, and your people will spread out over the mountains, without anyone gathering them.

There is no cure for your wound, your wound is painful. Everyone who hears your fame will clap your hands over you; why, on whom has your malice not continually passed?

Nahum 3: 13-19

This chapter of Nahum is related to Sephira Hod and the second Chakra called Swadhisthana in Sanskrit. It is little used, because being connected to the abyss it can bring energies from this place and evil spirits from the lower astral, be it Djinns or Dibbuks.

The church was in the abyss, as the Gentiles did not know the Creator and Yeshua's redemptive work took it out of the shadow of death and brought it into the light, all of this occurs in the human microcosm connected to the Splenic Chakra. On the other hand, people who do not follow the light will be shattered as they are in this passage of Nahum, by forces of chaos that will enter this vortex of energy and devour their lives.

Hod is not a negative energy vortex, all Sephira is positive, but for Hod to reach perfection, he must overcome the negative forces of the Splenic Chakra.

In the same way, no Chakra is negative; they are doors that can receive the energy of light or chaos. In this spleen chakra a powerful force from the abyss can manifest itself, but it can also be the place where darkness is overcome and the light begins to reign as it did with the church that was taken out of the darkness into the light with the spear that pierced the side. of the Messiah on Calvary.

Draw water for the siege, strengthen your strongholds; it enters the mud, and steps on the clay, takes the form for the bricks.

In the same way that the church was taken out of the void, the Splenic Chakra region is where the Creator works to make a temple in the middle of chaos. That's how he worked by putting a deep sleep on Adam and getting Eve off his rib.

It is in this place that the Creator creates the vessel that he works inside us, molding each cell, each atom, because as we know in the spleen many cells of the blood are formed and it is these cells that bring life to the body.

CHAPTER IV

THE UMBILICAL CHAKRA

Located two fingers below the navel, this Chakra is called the Manipura Chakra.

In Kabbalah the Chakra is represented by the Sephira Chesed. This Chakra in some schools is called the Umbilical Chakra and in others the Solar Plexus Chakra, but in fact it is located two fingers above the navel and not over the Navel and this is the Umbilical Chakra and the Splenic Chakra which is the solar plexus. But it is common to be confused because they are close and because there is another Chakra over the spleen.

The Chakra is called Manipura and is under the influence of the third dimension, which is the gross earth dimension, but in fact it is a dimension under strong infernal control.

While the spleen chakra is under control of the abyss, the umbilical chakra is under control of hell, so it is linked to our desires that become sin when we transgress the divine law. This Chakra is linked to Sephira Chesed, the Sephira of mercy. That is why I inverted and placed the umbilical chakra in third and not in second as in most schools, because the number 3 is the number of hell and this Chakra is connected to hell and the second chakra from the solar plexus to the abyss that is second dimension.

This Sephira is very important, because only when we use compassion for people, the mercy contained in it, do we begin to escape from darkness towards light, towards true life in the light of the Creator.

Chesed, the divine mercy in us makes us escape to the light, to the truth of the Creator, because we are stuck in matter and only when we use our souls to pray for other people interceding for them do we climb the tree of life.

The animal human being in his primitive instinct has no compassion, he does not care about the success of the other, and he aims only at the well being of him and his family as in prehistory. In order to rise to a new dimension of the soul, it is necessary to let go of this primitive instinct and develop our love and compassion for humanity.

This happens in Chesed.

As for the spleen chakra located near the solar plexus on the right, there is also the solar plexus chakra which is another. We have already said that there is also the umbilical chakra located on the navel, this on the navel is the true umbilical chakra connected to the 7 lower chakras that are infernal. Some esoteric schools set aside the Navel Chakra and replace it with the spleen on the right in the spear hole on Yeshua, as there is hellish pressure on the Chakra located on the navel.

Chesed acts on these two influences, both in the chakra on the navel which is located on the 7 lower belly chakras and also two fingers up on the spleen chakra which is more connected to the astral body and less connected to the infernal sphere.

In Chesed this transformation takes place, the infernal energy that bombards our umbilical chakra is modified when it reaches the spleen and the beings of darkness cannot pass to reach the heart, because in the compassion that is located over the spleen Chakra in Chesed we are able to transform the energy negative in emptiness and emptiness in light blocking the action of demons.

In Chesed there is a change from the primitive animal instinct to the higher instinct that feels compassion for others.

Buddhism fights a lot against the hatred, greed and illusion that are the cause of human misfortune and they are amplified in the umbilical chakra by poisoning man and leading man to hell, to be dominated by hell power.

When man practices certain barbaric crimes he is dominated by the infernal power, which arose from hatred, greed and illusion.

Not just crime, the domination of this infernal triad causes all kinds of sin and depravity. We have to block this infernal energy from the Draconian Sephiroth in the spleen, because in this place there is the transmutation of primitive man into an evolved man who lives under the control of the spiritual and not of the matter.

In short, the Umbilical Chakra is followed by 7 lower Chakras below it, which in some schools are 9 lower Chakras or 9 infernal or infernal spheres. The energy of the Shedim or demons comes through these 9 inferas and tries to enter our umbilical chakra to spread through the body. When we fast, pray, practice compassion or meditate, our body goes into a state of stillness and light and this prevents the strength of the Shedim from dominating our body.

CHAPTER V

THE HEART CHAKRA

This Chakra is over the heart, it is also invisibly linked to the energy channels to the limbic system in the brain from the heart, because in these places are our feelings, our way of seeing the world.

It is in the heart that we can decide our choices. Next to it is Daath, the Chakra of choice that makes us choose between good and evil, between the energy of light and that of darkness.

In this Chakra, the Dragon climbs the tree of life to offer us his kingdom, promising us glory and power. It is where we can choose good and evil, it is clear that evil is more tempting and comes to us in a garment that is difficult to reject.

The Dragon knows our weak point, our vices and passions and that is where he attacks us. It is difficult for those who manage to escape from their power, resist their beauty, sentimental and erotic beauty, taking the form of our beloved object, sexual object, whether male or female, as the case may be.

The Dragon knows how to hit us and with that we open our hearts to the Draconian Sephiroth that enters through the door of Daath and controls us.

Daath is not evil; it is just where we process our choices and where we take a stand before the world.

The energy of light and chaos is found in Daath and in this place is the balance of life, Menet, Menet, Tequel, Ufarsim, Adonai Menet Nut.

This Chakra is called Anahata by the Indians.

It is also through Anahata that all other connections on the three-dimensional plane occur: human beings, animals, plants and minerals.

The most important and most beautiful quality of Anahata Chakra is Bhakti: love and devotion.

Love and devotion manifest with understanding, acceptance, forgiveness, compassion and helpfulness.

The purer the Anahata Chakra, the deeper the feelings of joy, affection, happiness and oneness with everything and everyone is experienced.

When the Vishnu Granthi (a node located in the Anahata Chakra region) within the heart opens, the desire to help other living beings spontaneously arises. When entangled by Maya (illusion of separateness), man creates desires and needs according to his instincts and attachments and starts to select and create caught by the objects to be loved (my children, my friends, my house, my car, mine ,. my my).

Breaking the Vishnu Granthi leads to an open affective interaction, paving the way for Total Love that leads man to love everything and everyone indistinctly, fully and evenly expressing his emotions and dissolving his affective and relational breastplates.

Breaking the Vishnu Granthi also allows that no emotion experienced is repressed, on the contrary, that the emotion is perceived, that it feels, expresses itself and LET IT PASS ∞

When we are in Anahata Chakra our perceptions become more refined and comprehensive. Artistic talents and creative skills, through which we are able to touch the hearts of others, are awakened within us through the Anahata chakra.

Anahata Chakra is our inner temple in which the divine atman, "the flame of life", resides.

In Chandogya Upanishad it is written: "In the center of the body is a small altar surrounded by a wall with eleven doors. Hidden inside the sanctuary a lotus blooms, and inside it there is a small room "(which accesses Atma)

"The center of your heart is the place where life begins the most beautiful

Place on Earth "Rumi

The imbalance in Anahata leads to deceptive thoughts and feelings, fixed and complex ideas that affect us physically and psychologically.

Resentment, desire, obsession, fanaticism and dependence are negative qualities that cause corruption in Anahata Chakra.

http://yogi.somanatureza.com.br/2016/06/28/anahata-chakra/

This description of the beauty of this Chakra compared to the Lotus closes with the Sephira of Kabbalah attached to it, the Sephira Tifheret, right in the center of the body, right in the center of the tree of life.

Sephira Tifheret is also linked to the Messiah, the Messiah reigning in our lives when we accept him in our hearts. It was he who said that the door of our heart slams and when we open it we will have dinner with him and him with us.

Yeshua has always treated the heart as a house that can both shelter him and the forces of evil, it only depends on us.

We must decide whether to accept him or the forces of darkness.

The choice depends on us.

Tifheret is called the Christ center for some and is considered the most important because it is in the center of the body. It is there that we can choose between light and darkness and evolve or become trapped in darkness and death.

When Yeshua died, nature itself cried, but on the third day he rose from the dead and all nature, the whole cosmos filled with his beauty.

Thifereth is the beauty of Yeshua in every flower, in every bird, in every tree. It is his beauty when our soul is filled with joy and light before nature.

With his death nature went into mourning and the earth plunged into darkness. An unexplained eclipse happened everywhere, but in his resurrection nature and the world were filled with light.

Tifheret is the beauty that touches our hearts, nature is filled with life and light. And all of this is Anahata, the heart chakra, the connection with the infinite light, with the light of the Messiah.

CHAPTER VI

THE CHAKRA OF THE LARYNX

This Chakra is located on the larynx center of speech, something very important for the human being in the face of the cosmos. The larynx is in an important place, because it is with speech that we confess the Creator, that we praise him, it is also with him that we curse our neighbor and that we blaspheme against the divine.

In India this Chakra is called Vishuddha and covers the entire shoulder, jaw and neck, not just the larynx. He gets to the hearing, because speech and hearing are linked.

The 5th Chakra - Throat Chakra

POSTED ON AUGUST 11, 2012 BY LOTUS DE LAKSHIMI

His name, in Sanskrit, is Vishuddha, which means "The Purifier".

His color is Turquoise, Sky Blue.

His mantra is HAM.

His element is Ether, also being attributed to him in its most subtle form.

Crystals: Turquoise, Aquamarine, Blue Lace Agate and other stones in light blue color.

It is located, specifically in the throat region.

This chakra is directly linked to communication, verbal expression, creativity in the sense of knowing how to express oneself, the use of the word.

It also works as a bridge to the spirit world, because when it is open, communication becomes easy, fluent, and we often have difficulty being understood by old friends who, perhaps, are at a different stage of evolution, which means that the energies are being modified and that, consequently, they will attract new friends, according to the new vibration emitted.

When well balanced, our communication is facilitated, not only with people, but also with us, besides, of course, increasing our perception in the sense of telepathic communication. Our awareness is broadened, in the sense that we develop our responsibility in relation to our evolution and in relation to our material and spiritual needs.

By governing the thyroid, it has the function of purifying what we receive, before emitting, that is, the energies are purified before being emanated.

Physically, it governs the vocal cords, the thyroid, the throat, the mouth, nose and ears.

In disequilibrium, on an emotional level, it can cause communication and expression difficulties, anxiety, feeling of emptiness, stuttering. On the physical level: asthma, vertigo, allergies, anemia, fatigue, laryngitis, sore throat, cough, in addition to tendencies to respiratory and skin and thyroid problems.

To rebalance or keep it balanced, meditate in a peaceful and quiet place, using crystals and incense.

Here, techniques that refer to all elements and chakras are allowed, because Ether is Quintessence, the 5th element, the sum of all others. Techniques that use aromas (subtle, soft, such as jasmine, for example) are allowed, the elixirs based on one of the crystals above, and topaz, which is a stone governed by Mercury, responsible for Communication; besides, of course, outdoor walks, soft music, and, above all, deep reflection.

Reflect on the way you have communicated with people. Do you feel you have been talking too much? Do you feel so blocked that you can't say what you think should be said? Do you feel misunderstood, as if no one understands what you want to express?

Try not to keep it to yourself, try to speak at times when you must speak, using moderation, but also frankness. Sorrows can also unbalance this chakra, as a failure in communication between two people can cause friction or resentment. Observe the form that has been expressed.

Learn to speak, but also learn to listen. There is no communication without these two vehicles (speech and hearing) being used. In order to have a complete communication, it is necessary to know how to speak and to know how to listen. Every thing in its time.

Control anxiety. Things happen at the right time, neither before nor after. Accept the fact that everything has a natural course to follow.

Because it is also a chakra related to creativity, try to express yourself through creation, the arts, be they visual arts, music, poetry, theater, dance.

If you can't speak, if the moment doesn't allow for decisive conversation, where you can relieve yourself by saying what you have to say, write. Think of all the things you would like to say to someone and write them in a letter. At this point, it is up to you to decide whether or not to send it. Both options are valid, but if you choose not to send it, burn it and blow the ashes into the wind, imagining that the Universe is receiving your message and will serve you in a timely manner.

A great rebalancing technique consists of chanting the Ham mantra (pronouncing it with the open "A": HÁÁMMMMM), while letting one of the crystals described at the beginning of the post rest on your throat. Think of a Celestial Blue light coming out of you, turning it clockwise, activating this center and making it conducive to developing your functions on a regular basis.

Do this for 15 minutes a day and feel the difference!

https://lotusdelakshimi.wordpress.com/2012/08/11/o-4o-chakra-chakra-laringeo/

The Sephira of the tree of life attached to this Chakra is Gevurah which means strength and severity. This is because it is in speech that we have the power either for magic or to praise the Creator.

It is through speech that we also have the mantras of meditation, the key words that allow us to access the divine.

After this Sephiroth we have Chesed which is mercy and is in the center of the forehead or the third eye. Sephira Binah and Chokmah, understanding and wisdom symbolize the hemispheres right and left brain. Binah or understanding is what we call consciousness or the rational brain, the left side of the brain. Chokmah or wisdom is what has been kept in our brain for generations, what we call the subconscious. The Kether or crown is the seventh chakra at the top of the head, the crown chakra.

The larynx chakra works a lot with the left side of the brain or Binah, because when we speak we are acting in the world, building our space in the world. The right side of the brain is more subtle, more used in meditation.

Speech and hearing place us in this world, it is our reason for living, our capacity for action and reaction in this world, that is why they are so linked to consciousness.

We are a living organism taking our place in space, but there is a greater force that controls everything, the strength of the Creator.

It is he who leads us to pray, to cry out and with that we are sowing light into the world in a rational and conscious way.

When we meditate we are using Chokmah, the right side of the brain, which is more subtle but modest. When we speak we are using the laryngeal chakra with the understanding to control the world, to occupy our space in the world.

Meditation, however, leads us to a larger view of the universe, but it is with prayer, with speech that we dominate our negative selves and declare our victory.

It is also through it that we pray for souls trapped by the power of darkness.

CHAPTER VII

THE FRONT OR CHESED CHAKRA

The frontal chakra is in the center of the forehead and is connected to the pituitary or pituitary. This Chakra is called the third eye and is the main satellite of the Crown Chakra, the seventh Chakra at the top of the head that controls the entire body.

The third eye is the spiritual eye, the eye that we use when we are in the most subtle astral, vital or spiritual body.

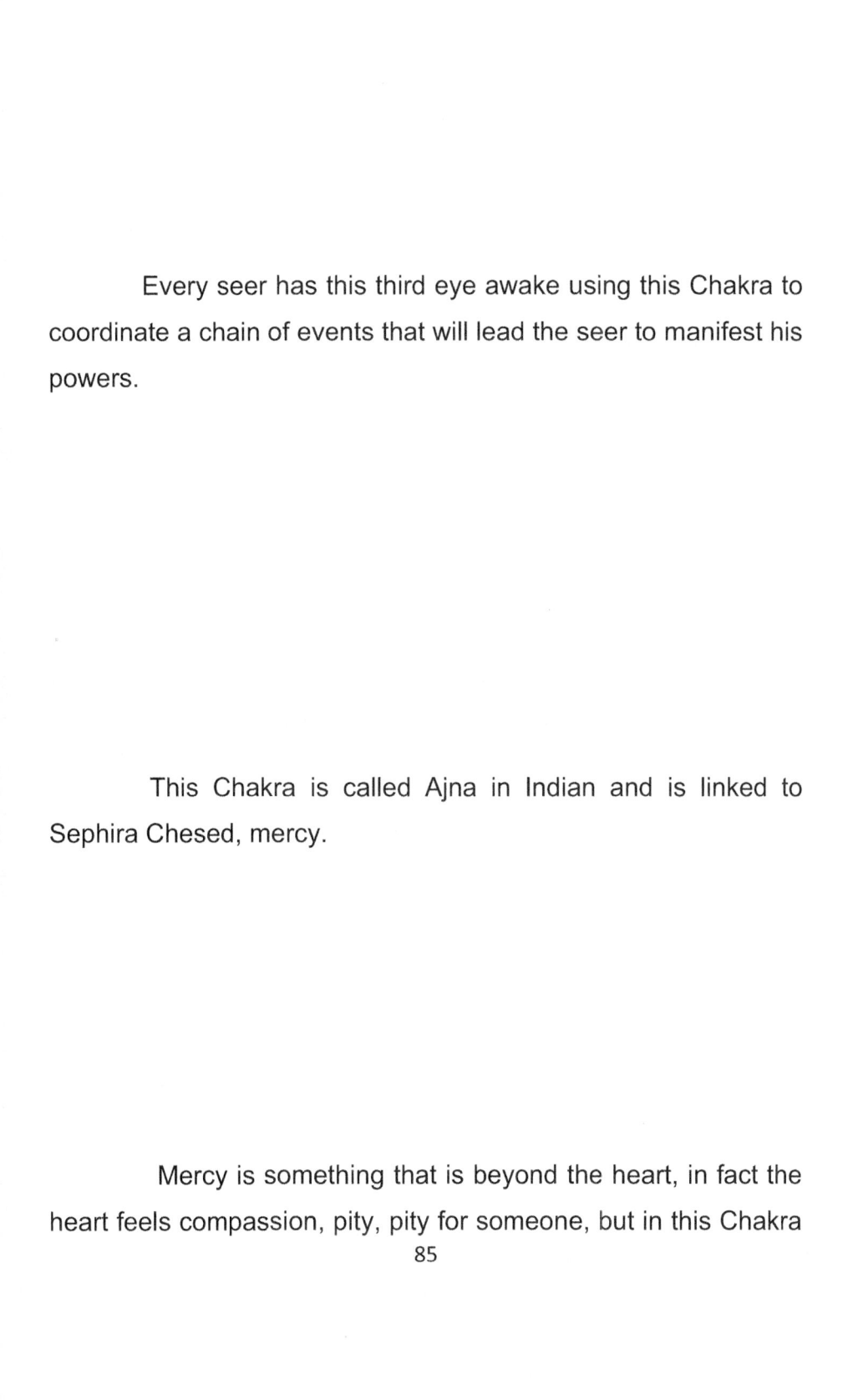

Every seer has this third eye awake using this Chakra to coordinate a chain of events that will lead the seer to manifest his powers.

This Chakra is called Ajna in Indian and is linked to Sephira Chesed, mercy.

Mercy is something that is beyond the heart, in fact the heart feels compassion, pity, pity for someone, but in this Chakra we feel mercy or Chesed, because it is more than compassion, it is suffering subconsciously for souls and that does not it occurs in the heart, it can only occur in this Chakra connected to the right hemisphere of the brain, the part of the brain connected to the etheric plane, creation, art, music, etc.

Chesed is more than simple mercy, it is when our mind traces something to bring light to a lost soul and it does not come from us, it is the Creator acting in our life.

In the third vision or the third eye, we can see the hidden and the hidden, and with that we can fight against the principalities that control the earth, that's why this Chakra is very attentive during meditation, shining its light splendidly.

Sephira Chesed feels the desire to share and intercede for trapped souls, she represents the one who has reached an optimal level of evolution and begins to make sacrifice for humanity.

Sacrifice for humanity is out of primitive, instinctive human behavior and is a light that shines in resonance with the Creator, for it is he who guides us to help souls trapped in chaos and darkness.

The third eye awakens our consciousness to the spirit, to something that is beyond matter. Although this Chakra is more connected to the subconscious, it also represents the development of a higher power or a consciousness linked to the sacred, the divine.

CHAPTER VIII

THE CORONARY CHAKRA

This Chakra is the most important, as it controls the central part of the brain and pineal gland. At Sephiroth he represents the highest degree, the Kether.

Sephira Binah and Chokmah, on the other hand, understanding and wisdom symbolize the right and left hemispheres of the brain. Binah or understanding is what we call consciousness or the rational brain, the left side of the brain. Chokmah or wisdom is what has been kept in our brain for generations, what we call the subconscious and whose main core is on the right side of the brain. The Kether or crown is the seventh chakra at the top of the head, the crown chakra.

The Kether forms with the Binah and Chokmah the golden triangle of human life control, radiating its power to the other energy vortexes of the body through the Sephira Chesed or third eye that serves as the expansion and command center of the Golden Triangle.

The crown chakra is the Creator's throne in us on top of the head and with the power of the pineal gland it controls everything.

The pineal gland is at the center of the human brain, at the very center just as Jerusalem is at the center of the world. It is shaped like a human eye and is one of the greatest symbols of the Egyptian religion in the remote past.

They already knew the powers of this gland over the human organism.

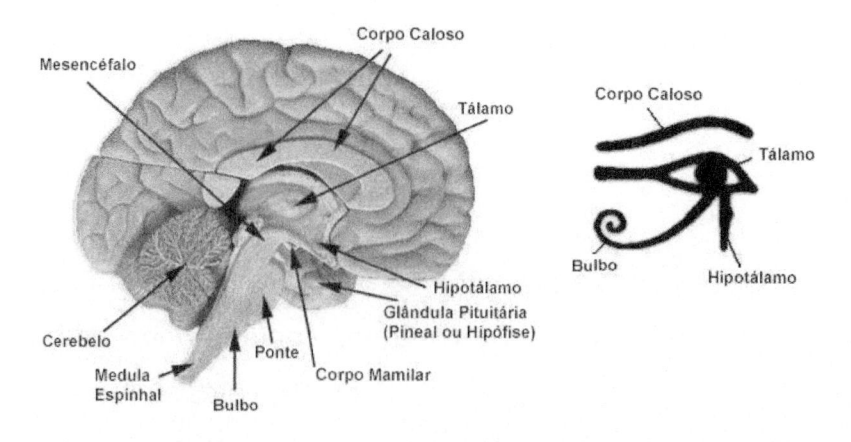

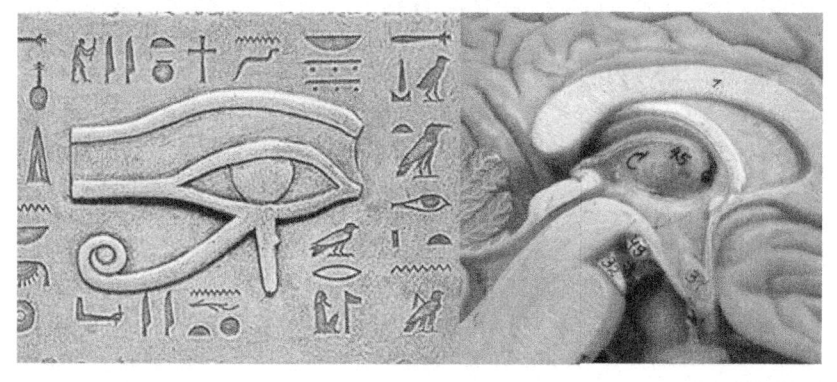

metanoian.wordpress.com fb.com/metanoian

http://www.guia.heu.nom.br/glandula_pineal.html

It is frightening the figure of this gland manifesting itself as our spiritual eye connecting us to the divine. This secret is fantastic. The pineal gland is big when we are children and our connection with the divine is open, pure, great, because of the child's purity, over time it will decrease and become the size of a wrinkled pea.

This gland appears a lot in the brain's resonance, because many apatite crystals appear in it in the resonance. These crystals happen when the gland is calcified according to some, for others the crystals help in the communication with the divine, because they reflect the electromagnetic energy of the divine in the physical.

The spiritual plane is full of power and energy and controls the physical. We, mere mortals, cannot see these beings around us in the invisible manifest, but if the pineal gland is developed it can capture this energy from parallel worlds, these beings from other worlds, whether they be light or dark.

Kabbalists and Talmudists know that good and evil, light energies and chaos energies can pass through this gland, so they created the Kipa, the Jewish prayer cap as head protection against the Shedim and also like to use the talit, the Jewish prayer cloak with which they cover their heads in prayer.

With that they are shielded against the energies of chaos and are able to communicate directly with the divine.

The ways in which Jews pray by rocking the body back and forth also have a connection with the pineal gland, because in this act of rocking the body they activate the pineal by releasing melatonin throughout the body.

Melatonin is a hormone secreted by the pineal gland and released into the body. This hormone makes our body relax by bringing sleep. Without it we would not be able to sleep and would go crazy.

Restful sleep only happens when melatonin is released into the body. Scientists have found that the more darkness of the night the more melatonin is released and the body is relaxed, which is why sleeping at night is so important. Whoever works at night knows that daily sleep is not the same thing, the person is always tired.

Melatonin is also released in meditation and with that the body enters a state of total relaxation. It is at night and with the great release of melatonin that our mind enters the world of dreams, in the empirical world, living fantastic experiences.

This shows the total and direct link between the sleep world, the empirical world and the pineal gland that generates this hormone.

The ancient Shamans always believed that dreams were doors to the divine, entered into parallel spiritual worlds and indeed dreams are brain generations of events in the etheric or spiritual worlds. Our spirit and our soul interact with etheric dimensional worlds and the way they find to pass the messages of the world from there to us is through the dream.

This process is possible with the participation of melatonin, releasing relaxation on the body, also because the pineal gland is a direct link with the etheric world.

The images captured from the spiritual world pass through the pineal gland and spill over the brain to form dreams. Dreams form at the back of the brain, deep inside. The cerebral cortex is also activated when the dream occurs.

It is important to point out that dreams integrate the organism as a whole and happen not only in the brain, but also in other chakras in the organism, but it is in the pineal gland, in the coronary chakra that the energy is poured out first and then spreading to the other centers sensory effects of the body.

Today synthetic melatonin is sold, but it can be obtained naturally in meditation. We said that melatonin has more effect at night, but it can be produced at all times, when we meditate we are producing melatonin and releasing it in the body, increasing immunity, fighting cancer, aging and various forms of disease.

The Kether or coronary chakra is directly connected to the pineal gland, radiating its energy over it.

It is necessary to know the pineal gland so that we can understand our organism and understand the Sephira Kether, the throne of the Creator in the microcosm of our body. A reflection of the Creator's throne at the center of the universe.

I want to highlight here the power of the right and left hemisphere of the brain, Chokmah and Binah, forming the golden triangle with the pineal where the crown is in the Crown Chakra.

The power of these 3 energy vortexes is incredible and when they work in harmony form the pyramid of eternal life, the Golden Triangle. In meditation it is possible to connect these 3 forces forming a pyramid of mental and spiritual power.

CHAPTER IX

MEDITATION TO ACTIVATE THE PINEAL GLAND AND CORONARY CHAKRA

Sit in silence in the most serene part of your house, on the floor, yes, on the ground in contact with the energy of the earth. Start to suck in the air through your nose and release through your mouth.

Breathe a little while letting your mind calm down, then when you release the air, pronounce the expression Kether Hashem.

Kether is the crown of Sephiroth; it is where the pineal gland is in the human microcosm, archetype of the divine. Hashem is one of the titles for the Eternal, that is to say the one that has the name, in reference to the tetragramatom. As I mentioned above, the Kether Chakra, Crown, speaks of the Father, of the Creator of everything that is why uniting Kether and Hashem is talking about the same attunement.

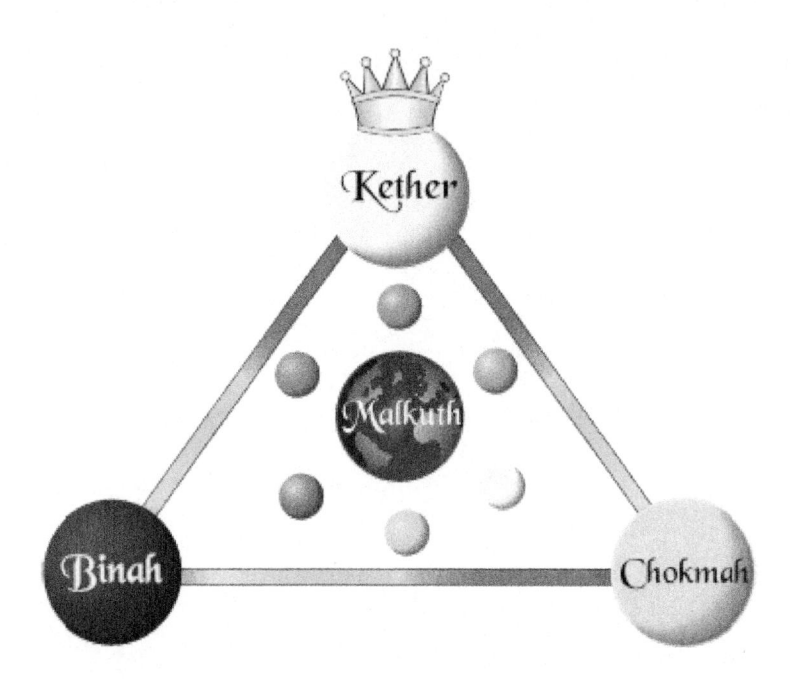

http://muitoalem2013.blogspot.com.br/2015/12/trindades.html

After a while of practicing this meditation imagine a powerful light coming from the Creator and entering the top of your head, filling your whole being.

Imagine this light coming straight down from the Creator's throne, shining more than a thousand suns.

It enters the pineal, at the top of your head and manifests itself throughout the body; it spreads throughout the body like water flowing from the waterfall.

Just as the water flows in the waterfall, the light flows from the Father coming to you.

Practice this meditation ten minutes every day and soon you will see miracles happening.

CONCLUSION

Indian science is totally linked to Kabbalah and the 7 Chakras are part of the human archetype in relation to the divine and the cosmos.

Binah as the left hemisphere of the brain and Chokmah as the right hemisphere complete this magical scheme of Sephiroth and its connection with our body.

Whoever receives the divine father in his soul receives his light, his power, but many today deny him and receive the suspicious light from inferior forces that seek to control humanity.

Open your mind to the divine father by repeating this prayer with me:

Divine Father through your son Yeshua I receive your light in my life, let it descend through the Crown or Kether of my head and spread throughout my body making me resonate with a unique piece of light and radiator of peace.

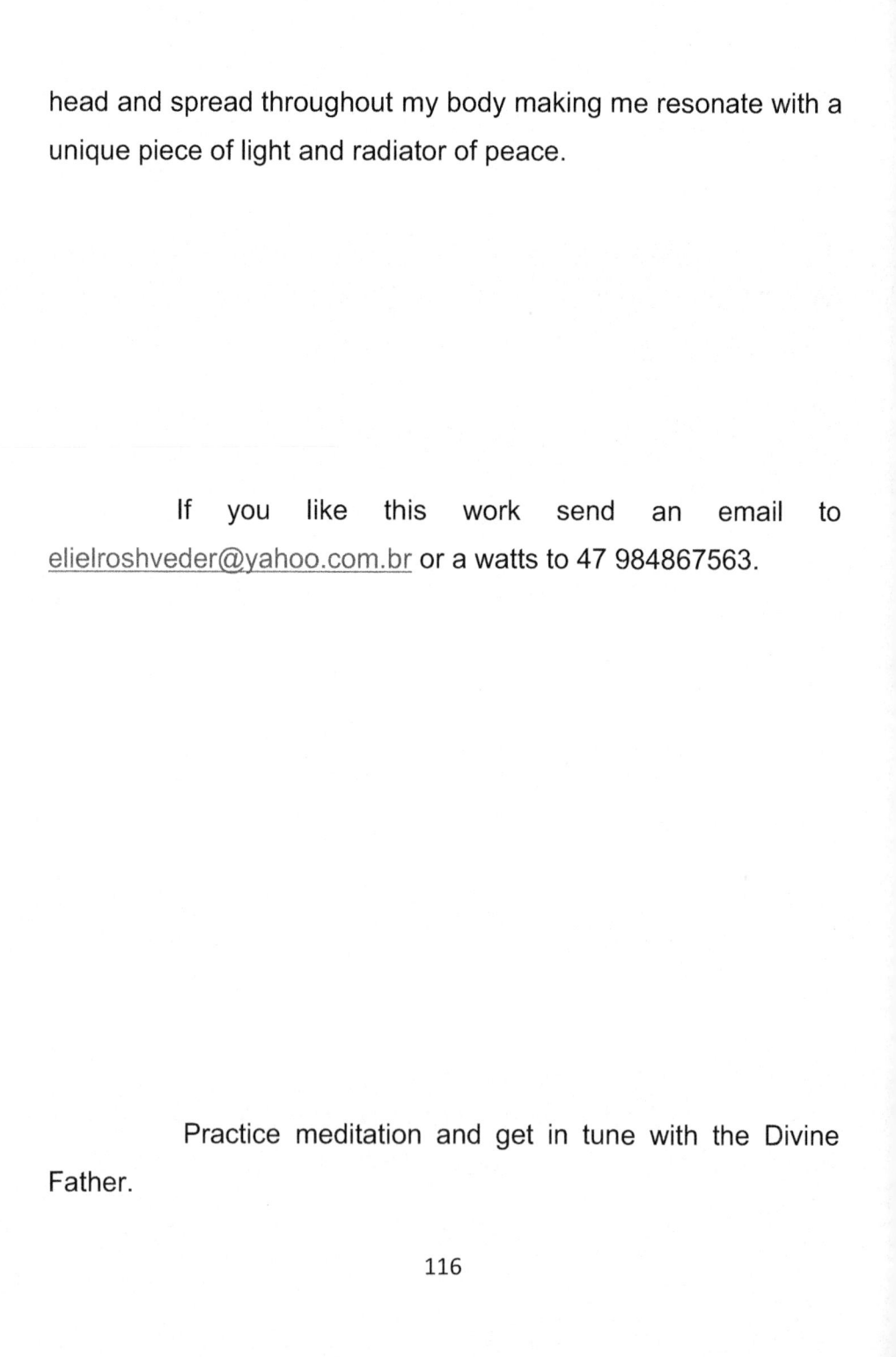

If you like this work send an email to elielroshveder@yahoo.com.br or a watts to 47 984867563.

Practice meditation and get in tune with the Divine Father.

Printed in Great Britain
by Amazon